To

With [illegible] regards.

Michael J. Tyler is a Senior Lecturer in the Department of Zoology at the University of Adelaide, and is also Chairman of the Board of the South Australian Museum. He is the author of four other books and more than 150 scientific papers on frogs. For the past few years he has led teams of zoologists into northern Australia at the height of each wet season which has resulted in the discovery of dozens of new species. His laboratory research has centred upon the Gastric Brooding Frog and on the use of frogs in environmental monitoring.

THERE'S A FROG IN MY ~~THROAT~~ STOMACH

MICHAEL J. TYLER

COLLINS
Sydney

Published 1984 by William Collins Pty Ltd, Sydney
Typeset by Post Typesetters, Brisbane
Printed and bound by Globe Press, Melbourne

National Library of Australia
Cataloguing-in-Publication data

Tyler, Michael J., 1937—
There's a frog in my throat stomach.

Title appears with 'throat' crossed out and 'stomach' substituted.
Bibliography.
ISBN 0 00 217321 2.

1. Rheobatrachus silus. 2. Frogs — Australia.

592.8'9

CONTENTS

Preface

Frogs are rather special animals to us. We can eat them—either real frogs or else chocolate or cake effigies of them. We can make models of them—in gold, silver, brass, copper, pewter, glass, ivory, wood, plastic . . . in fact, anything that takes our fancy. We can discover them in cartoons, in songs or poems. And (understandably) we can read books about them, or even write one if so moved.

This is a little book about a particularly special kind of Australian frog. It is known by its Latin name, *Rheobatrachus silus*, and by the common names 'Gastric Brooding Frog' or 'Platypus Frog'. What makes this rare frog so noteworthy is that the mother swallows her young, broods them in her stomach and eventually gives birth to them through her mouth. This isn't unique just for a frog; it's unique in the entire Animal Kingdom.

The Gastric Brooding Frog was first found in 1972. It was given its name in 1973, and its weird reproductive habits were discovered in the following year. And as more and more discoveries about the frog are being made all the time, public interest and concern for its future has not stopped growing. Requests for further information come to me with increasing frequency. People either want answers to specific questions, or else they want to know where they can read a complete account on this special frog.

Although there is a technical book on the frog, which has just been published (for details see page 49), there is little material which is suitable for the naturalist or the high school student. This book attempts to fill the gap. It contains a summary of what is known about the natural history of the Gastric Brooding Frog, and of the changes that take place in its stomach to suit it for the new role of housing tadpoles and baby frogs. Details of some of the research currently being undertaken are also included.

The line illustrations are the work of Ruth Hughes. Photographs are acknowledged with the captions to the plates. I take this opportunity to thank all my colleagues for their contributions. This is also an opportunity to thank the Utah Foundation, The University of Adelaide, the Australian Research Grants Scheme, The Savings Bank of South Australia, the Mark Mitchell Foundation and the many individuals whose grants and donations made the research possible.

CHAPTER 1

The World of Frogs

Compared with many other kinds of animals, frogs give the impression of being rather conservative creatures. Frogs have existed on the earth for almost 200 million years. However, even after such a huge time span they have retained a body form which is basically no different from that of their ancestors. In contrast, mammals have existed for only half that period, but now they are represented by animals as widely different from one another as the shrew, the bat and the whale.

Frogs, nevertheless, do not have a monopoly on evolutionary conservatism. In sheltered, stable environments some other animals have similarly diverged very slightly from the form of their ancestors. For example, the Coelacanth, that ancient fish of the deep waters off the coast of East Africa, has a skeleton which is strikingly like the fossils of ancestral forms that existed 300 million years ago. This is why people sometimes refer to the modern Coelacanth as a 'living fossil'. The dark, cold, high-pressured abyssal depths of the oceans are unlikely to experience much change over long periods of time, and so a species which is adapted perfectly to a life there is also unlikely to change.

But frogs, unlike the Coelacanth, have not lived in sheltered environments. The world's climate and vegetation have altered enormously since they made their first appearance. Tropical zones have become temperate; temperate zones have changed to arid deserts; and sub-tropical forests have been covered by glaciers. Rainfall and temperature have fluctuated wildly. Seas have risen to flood the land and have then fallen again, or else they have fallen to create new land connections. Mountains have risen 6,000 metres. And all throughout this huge environmental upheaval frogs have survived. They have even flourished, establishing colonies in all areas of the earth except the icy wastes of the poles. Now, after 200 million years, they are still frogs.

But although the skeleton of frogs appears to be conservative, the soft parts of their body are not. It is remarkable that frogs have not been in any way constrained by their skeleton, and this is shown by their numerous and remarkable adaptations. As the first vertebrates to colonize the land, the majority of species of frogs throughout the world remained (understandably) principally terrestrial, occupying the area at the base of vegetation and beneath leaf litter and similar debris. Nevertheless there are numerous arboreal and fossorial (burrowing) species, and a few more species are aquatic. Altogether, at least 3,200 species of frogs are currently known, and probably some 500 more species are awaiting discovery.

To make generalizations about frogs, even in the case of those frogs that have fundamental similarities in terms of where they spend most of their lives, is to risk falling into the trap of oversimplification. However, the truth of the matter is that similarities do exist—for instance in problems of survival, such as avoiding being eaten by snakes at the edge of pools, which applies irrespective of whether the frogs are in Malaysia, in Zambia or anywhere else. Similarly, species of frogs which live in areas that experience seasonal droughts share the same problems, irrespective of which country or continent they happen to be in. In fact, one of the really remarkable features about frogs is precisely the resemblance of their adaptations to similar habitats. This capacity of frogs to independently develop similar adaptations in a wide variety of lifestyles provides one of the best examples of evolutionary convergence.

There is probably more variation in body form amongst those species that live at ground level than amongst arboreal or aquatic species. One of the successful models is that of the longest limbed frogs, which are all ground-dwelling species. These frogs are disadvantaged in that they have a particularly high ratio of surface area to body volume, and so they have a greater surface area from which they can lose water. This rate of water loss is a luxury that can only be indulged in if such ground-dwelling species have ready access to moisture in order to replenish the lost body water. On the other hand, the evolution of long limbs improves a frog's leaping ability. Therefore it has a better chance to escape from predators such as the wading birds, the snakes and the rats that search for them at the water's edge.

Long limbs thus have to be viewed as highly advantageous in the particular habitat of ground-dwelling frogs. But, because of the unfavourable surface-volume ratio, they can be disadvantageous elsewhere. This is therefore an adaptation which goes wholly against the overall trend of frogs becoming less dependent upon water.

Another adaptation is that of the so-called poison arrow frogs of Central and South America, which are best known for the variety of toxins secreted by their skins, and also for the brilliant colours by which they warn potential predators to keep clear. Some of these frogs are unusual also in their ability to move around on four limbs with the body raised up and off the ground. Elaborate fights can occur between the males—they stand erect, their hindlimbs extended, grappling each other with their arms.

Terrestrial species that have moved further from the water include the rough-skinned toads (*Bufo*). In their case, the skin of the back is thickened and appears warty, and many species have very large, protruding parotoid glands of venom on their shoulders (Plate 1). The thick skin no doubt reduces water loss, but as the skin of frogs also serves as a respiratory surface from which oxygen is absorbed and carbon dioxide is released, the thickening of the skin will almost certainly impair that gas exchange. It would be interesting therefore to discover whether the lungs of these toads are more highly developed so as to compensate for the reduced efficiency of the skin.

The physical step from a terrestrial life to one in which the frog burrows underground to avoid periods of arid conditions is not too substantial. Some *Bufo* try to burrow by scraping with their hind feet and pushing backwards to get beneath debris, but most truly fossorial species have reduced hind legs, and a semi-circular disc (called a scaphoid or modified inner metatarsal tubercle) on the undersurface at the base of the first toe. By shuffling they scrape the soil with their special tubercle and so descend bottom first into the soil. The best known examples of bottom-first burrowers are the *Scaphiopus* species in North America and the *Cyclorana* species (water-holding frogs) of the arid zones of central and northern Australia.

There are also a few species of frogs which burrow with their hands, such as the *Copiula* species in New Guinea, and the recently discovered *Arenophryne rotunda* which inhabits coastal sandhills in Western Australia (Plate 2). These species enter the soil head first and in fact always have a pale patch of dead tissue upon the tips of their snouts like a callus on a foot! This patch protects the living tissue beneath.

Whilst beneath the ground, fossorial frogs secrete from the skin a cocoon around their bodies. This resembles a transparent and rather crisp cellophane bag (Plate 3). It is composed of dead skin which, instead of being shed and then eaten in one piece in the fashion of most frogs, forms a loose sheath around the individual. Water loss through the cocoon is less than through living skin, but this is probably of little significance because, almost inevitably, the soil in which the frogs burrow retains moisture.

The so-called tree frogs (Plate 4) for their part exhibit a suite of characteristics suitable for climbing and for resting vertically—either in vegetation or (if they so choose) upon artificial structures such as vertical sheets of glass. The most conspicuous of their adaptive features is the way in which the ends of their fingers and toes are expanded into circular, flattened discs. When the surface of these discs is examined under a scanning electron microscope, the individual cells on the undersurface are seen to be separated from one another by spaces (Plate 5). The spaces lead to glands situated deeper in the disc, which secrete an adhesive substance and which provide a means for the adhesive to ooze up to the surface. Of equal importance here are the ways the frog has of increasing the area of its body that can come into contact with the surface upon which it rests. For example, the skin of the abdomen is loose: when pressed against a smooth surface it excludes all air, thus increasing the contact and enabling the surface tension to assist adhesion (Plate 6).

In water, frogs, tadpoles and spawn are eaten by rats, wading

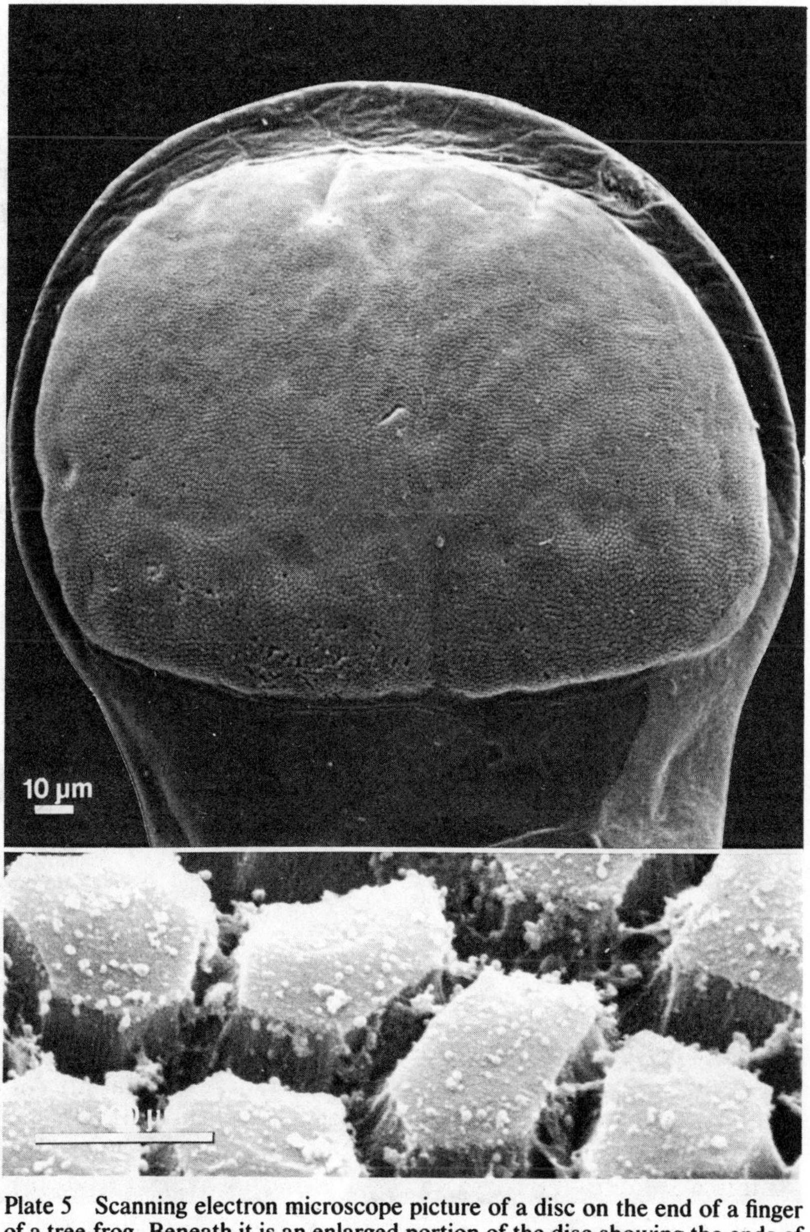

Plate 5 Scanning electron microscope picture of a disc on the end of a finger of a tree-frog. Beneath it is an enlarged portion of the disc showing the ends of the separate cells. (C. Miller)

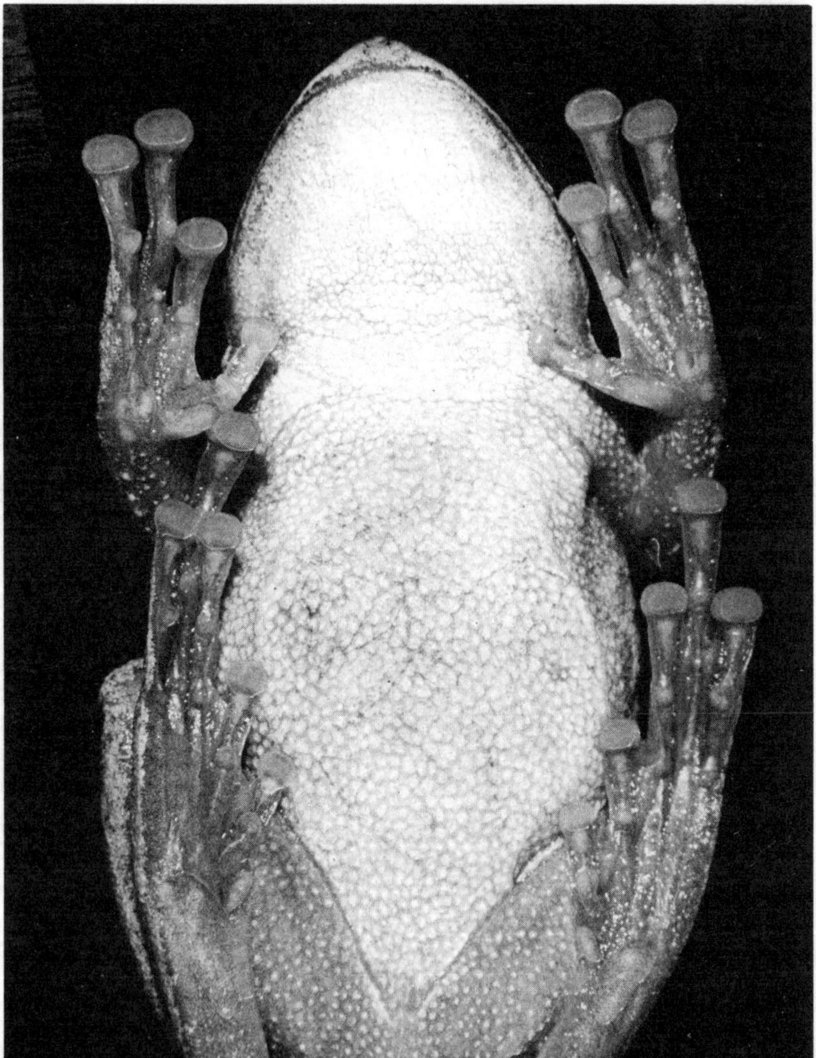

Plate 6 A tree frog at rest on a sheet of glass. Note the way in which the skin is flattened closely against the surface. (B. Stankewytsch-Janusch)

birds, snakes, turtles, water beetles, water bugs and spiders—to list just a few of their predators. In general, frogs have not developed defence strategies that are effective in water. Perhaps this is because their entire evolutionary trends have been towards becoming as independent as possible from water, and now many species no longer return to water to breed. It is hardly surprising therefore to discover that there are very few species that remain predominantly aquatic.

The best known example from amongst the few aquatic frogs that exist is the African Clawed Frog *Xenopus laevis*, which is also maintained throughout the world as a laboratory animal. This frog is very slimy. It retains a lateral-line sensory system which consists of rows of sense organs situated on the sides of the head and body and across the chest and throat. The lateral-line organs function as an early warning detection system, monitoring any movement created in the vicinity of the frog. The same detection system occurs in fishes and in many tadpoles, but it is extremely rare in adult frogs.

Another African aquatic frog is *Hymenochirus*. This species shares with *Xenopus* the adaptation of unusual feet with widely spread toes linked by extensive webbing. Such webbing is not unique to aquatic frogs but it is certainly better developed by them. When the toes are spread apart fully, the surface area of the foot is substantial, thus assisting the thrust of the frog through water.

In Australia there is a single species of aquatic frog. Like *Xenopus* it has a slimy skin and also a row of tiny lumps on the side of the body that probably constitute sensory organs of some kind. The foot too is extensively webbed. This species is *Rheobatrachus silus*, but it is not renowned for its aquatic adaptations. Of far greater interest is its unique habit of swallowing its fertilized eggs, of rearing its tadpoles in its stomach, and finally of giving birth to baby frogs through its mouth. This is the frog known as the 'Gastric Brooding Frog' or 'Platypus Frog'.

CHAPTER 2

Frog Reproduction

The fundamental characteristics of the reproduction of frogs are described in most books as a return of adults to water, where they lay their eggs. The eggs hatch and develop firstly into swimming tadpoles and then progressively into frogs.

Hence frogs are considered to have an existence that can be divided conveniently into first an aquatic life and then a terrestrial (or otherwise non-aquatic) period. This explains their classification as Amphibia, a word derived from 'Amphi' meaning 'double' and 'bios' or 'life'. Describing the migration of adults to water as a 'return' to that site is telling because it emphasizes the traditional view that frogs are still dependent upon water for breeding purposes. This is despite their evolutionary successes upon land, which then have to be viewed simply as the colonizing of a hostile environment. We are thus led to believe that frogs just cannot break these last historical ties with water.

But the reality is a little different. Many hundreds of species do not breed in water at all but instead lay their eggs in sites that are just exposed to moisture. A large proportion of these species has totally eliminated the free-swimming tadpole stage. The embryo develops within egg membranes upon land and emerges as a perfectly formed frog. In yet other species the embryos are transported by one or other of the parents, occasionally in a manner that vaguely resembles that of the marsupials. On many, many occasions various species of frogs have separately evolved very neat ways of becoming independent of water for breeding. The Gastric Brooding Frog represents the most bizarre of these results. To place it in perspective, however, it is necessary to review the reproduction of other species.

Species that breed in static water, for instance, tend to lay large numbers of small eggs, which are often little more than one millimetre in diameter. As the eggs are so small each individual tadpole is provided with very little yolk. Hence its early development is dominated by the need to rapidly construct mouthparts and a gut so as to digest food and to eliminate the waste material left behind. This early activity of locating and digesting food material is retained as the tadpole grows, and indeed it becomes the predominant activity throughout the tadpole's life.

In contrast, species that breed out of water lay larger eggs, and in general the size of the egg is an indication of the degree of independence which has been inherited by the developing embryo. The larger the yolk sac with which the embryo is equipped, the longer it can defer seeking food and so devote its energy entirely to differentiation. In some extreme cases the yolk sac can be wholly sufficient for the entire period of embryonic growth. For the sake of convenience each of these different strategies is considered separately below.

Many species have quite independently of one another evolved the habit of delaying the emergence of the tadpole from the egg membranes that surround it. A few species of tree frogs on several continents, such as *Centrolenella valerioi* of South America and *Litoria iris* of New Guinea, lay them on leaves overhanging water. The tadpoles hatch from the surrounding membranes at a slightly later stage than if the eggs are laid in static water, and so they are fitter, stronger, more agile and better able to cope with flowing water—in which a younger and less well developed tadpole could easily be swept away.

This strategy of 'delayed emergence' (from the egg membranes) is also practised by the Australian species of *Pseudophryne*, which, instead of laying eggs on leaves of trees above flowing water, lays them simply on the ground. Following heavy autumn rains that dampen the baked soils, the *Pseudophryne* species lays the eggs beneath leaves and other debris. The frogs commonly select slight depressions in the soil (including those created by the hooves of horses) or else in cracks. The eggs develop slowly and eventually the tadpoles halt their development altogether. Further heavy rains after several weeks (or even sometimes as much as three months) trigger the tadpoles in some way and they move vigorously and split the membranes around them. As they hatch they are washed into the nearest pond where they complete their development in the customary fashion.

There are many examples of delayed emergence, including species that delay the release of tadpoles from spawn laid in water. However, the eggs laid on land seem to be a perfect intermediate stage towards the ultimate adaptation of complete independence from water. Tadpoles in this way spend their entire period of development within the egg membranes: they have no free-swimming tadpole stage and instead they emerge as perfectly formed miniature frogs (Figure 1). This process of development entirely within the egg membranes is termed 'direct development'. Species exhibiting this reproductive strategy occur commonly in areas of very high rainfall where the soils fail to retain free water in pools, or else where the ground is steeply sloping and thus where the only water is in the form of torrents.

By human standards most frogs are bad parents. To simply abandon early embryonic offspring in water does not seem to be the height of parental care. Frequently the frogs do not even make any assessment as to whether the water body in which they deposit the spawn will persist for some time so as to permit the young to complete their development. I have found spawn in a shallow puddle in the middle of the road! But if frogs could make an assessment of the human species, they might well suggest that for two adults to spend one third of their lifespan tending (often with limited ultimate success) just one individual offspring is little for humans to boast about. No doubt there are pitfalls in making assessments of the habits of animals which pre-suppose that humans are the ultimate achievers in this field.

In fact, many species of frogs exhibit a degree of parental care, with associated structural and physiological adaptations, that are astounding by any standards. Although it is the norm for adult frogs to abandon their spawn, in a few species the adults remain to guard the eggs, or else they take similar fundamental steps that will assist the survival of their offspring. For example, the male of the giant

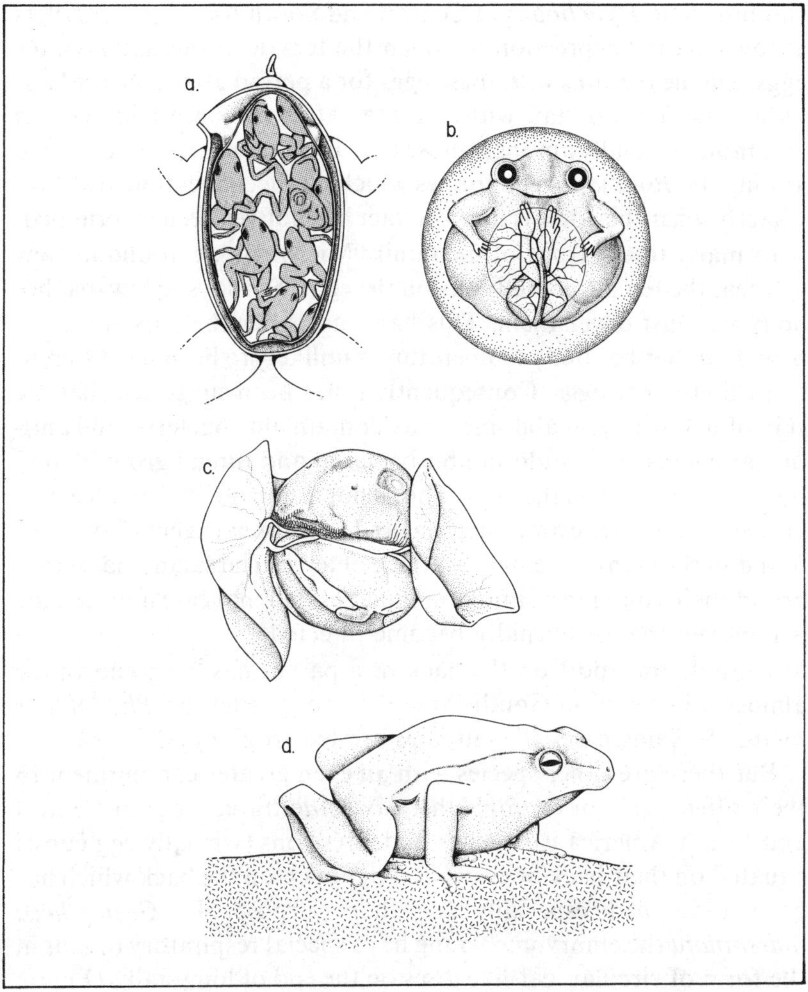

Figure 1 Unusual forms of development **(a)** *Rhinoderma darwini* of Chile. The male parent carries young in his vocal sac. In this figure the skin and the outer wall of the enlarged vocal sac have been removed to reveal the young. (After Howes, 1888, Proc. Zool. Soc. London, p. 233, Fig. 2) **(b)** Juvenile of a New Guinea frog developing inside the egg capsule. (After Mehely, 1901, Termeszetr. Fuz. 24, Table 9) **(c)** Developing young of *Gastrotheca marsupiata* which have bell-shaped gills. (After Noble, 1927, Ann. New York Acad. Sci. 30, Fig. 22, p. 94) **(d)** Adult male *Assa darlingtoni* of Australia which has hip pouches in which it carries its young.

climbing frog *Hyla boans* of Central and South America constructs a bowl-shaped depression in which the female eventually lays her eggs, and he remains with these eggs for a period after they are laid. Other species too stay with the eggs after they are laid. This is common especially amongst those that are laid on land, for example among the *Pseudophryne* species which has been mentioned above. Exactly what the adult is doing in fact has not yet been determined.

In many of the frogs of the family Microhylidae, found in New Guinea, the female actually sits on the eggs. She lays so few that her body will just cover them. This habit gives her the appearance of brooding, but her body temperature is unlikely to be much different from that of the eggs. Consequently it has been suggested that the skin of her chest and abdomen may contain anti-bacterial and anti-fungal agents that could inhibit bacterial and fungal growth upon the jelly which coats the eggs. This is not as far-fetched an idea as it may sound, because anti-bacterial and anti-fungal agents have been found in the skin of the undersurface of terrestrial salamanders that brood their young in a similar manner, and in that case if the female is removed the eggs rapidly become infected.

Tadpole transport on the back of a parent has been known for almost 130 years in South American frogs such as *Phyllobates pictus*. In some cases the tadpoles are fed frog's eggs.

But there are other species with an even greater commitment to their offspring. For example the *Gastrotheca* tree frogs of Central and South America carry eggs in depressions (virtually egg cups!) situated on their back or else in a skin pouch on the back which has been developed especially for that purpose. In *Gastrotheca marsupiata* the embryonic young have special respiratory organs in the form of circular leaf-like discs on the end of long stalks (Figure 1c).

The fact that the skin of *Gastrotheca* is modified to assist the developing young is of course remarkable, but it is nothing compared with the degree of change which is exhibited by the tiny rainforest frog *Assa darlingtoni* of Queensland, Australia. The male of this species has hip pockets into which the hatching tadpoles wriggle, and he transports them in these pockets for the entire period of their development (Figure 1d). As they grow they occupy more and more space, squashing the male's own internal organs to such an extent that eventually his stomach is pushed flat and he cannot feed. Perhaps this is the true meaning of the expression 'a glutton for punishment'.

Until recently the ultimate refinement in frog parental care was thought to be in the activities of the males of *Rhinoderma darwini*, found in Chile and a small portion of Argentina. In that species the young tadpoles 'swim' into the mouth of the male and push their way, via small apertures located on each side of the tongue, into the vocal sac located in the throat. Normally the vocal sac of male frogs is used as a resonance chamber to amplify sounds produced by the larynx. The sac is inflated during calling and often it is stretched into a vast, protruding bag.

This ability of the vocal sac to increase in size is ideal for its conversion to a brood sac for the young. Figure 1a is from a sketch published in 1888. It shows the way in which the vocal sac grows and protrudes into the space between the skin and the underlying muscles of the throat and abdomen. In *Rhinoderma darwini* eventually the fully developed young frogs leave the father via the apertures in the floor of his mouth, whilst he considerately opens his mouth wide.

The discovery that the Australian frog *Rheobatrachus silus* could give birth to live young through its mouth was made in 1973. It led to the obvious initial assumption that here was an example of evolutionary convergence with *Rhinoderma darwini*, and that *Rheobatrachus* similarly carried its young in its vocal sac. Within three weeks of the initial observation, however, came the astonishing finding that the frog was not a male with a vocal sac at all, but instead a female without one—and that the babies developed in the mother's stomach!

CHAPTER 3

The Gastric Brooding Frog

The Gastric Brooding Frog is so different from any other species in the world in as far as its involvement in parental care is concerned that it comes as somewhat of a surprise to discover that it is by no means a spectacular species of frog to look at. In reality it is a small frog which ranges in colour from dull brown (like the individual in Plate 7) to a drab slate. Since television has enabled us to view the most glorious creatures on earth we have come to expect high standards, and against these *Rheobatrachus* scarcely merits a second glance.

What is astounding is the fact that the females are at most only little more than 50 millimetres long.* People comment frequently that they had expected the species to be much larger. The female just doesn't seem big enough to carry babies in her stomach. The size range of females is 44–54 mm and that of males is 33–41 mm.

The most striking feature of *Rheobatrachus* is that its eyes are unusually prominent and located high upon the flattened head. As a result the eyes appear to protrude upwards like those of crocodiles. And indeed, like the crocodile, *Rheobatrachus* is in fact an aquatic animal that can rest with just the tip of its snout and the eyes above the surface of the water.

The skin is slimy and rather rough upon the back but quite smooth beneath. When the skin of the back is examined under an electron microscope, narrow channels can be detected upon the surface, particularly upon the flanks (Plate 8). The function of these channels has not yet been ascertained but it has been suggested that they serve to prevent dehydration when the frogs are out of water by

*The length of frogs is measured with a pair of callipers from the tip of the snout to the cloaca (vent) at the end of the body.

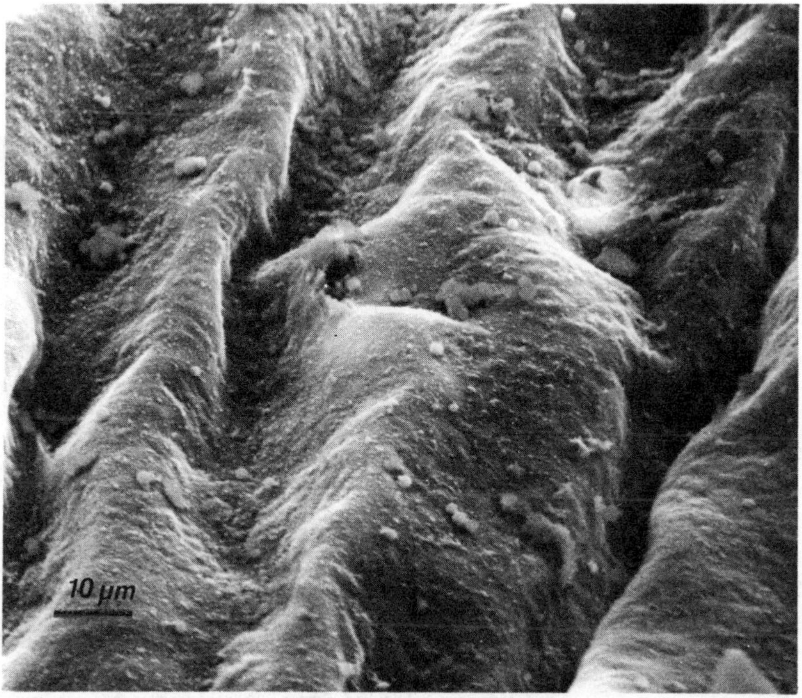

Plate 8 Scanning electron microscope picture of external surface of skin of *Rheobatrachus silus* showing longitudinal grooves upon surface. (C. Miller)

drawing water across the surface in a capillary column. Some of the rough areas on the back and on the limbs are due to the presence of raised wart-like structures. Whereas human warts are abnormal growths that are irregular in their form, these raised areas on the back of the frogs (termed tubercles) are elevated hills of cells commonly symmetrical in form and stacked up like piles of sandbags. These mounds are sense organs of unknown function. There are also some elongate, spire-shaped skin growths; and the sensory function of these structures also is unknown (Plate 9).

The skin of frogs is a complex tissue which is involved in protection, cooling, respiration and elimination of waste material. In all species there are two different kinds of skin glands:

A. *Mucous Glands*—these secrete mucus in order to cool the skin, and hence the animal, by evaporation; also in order

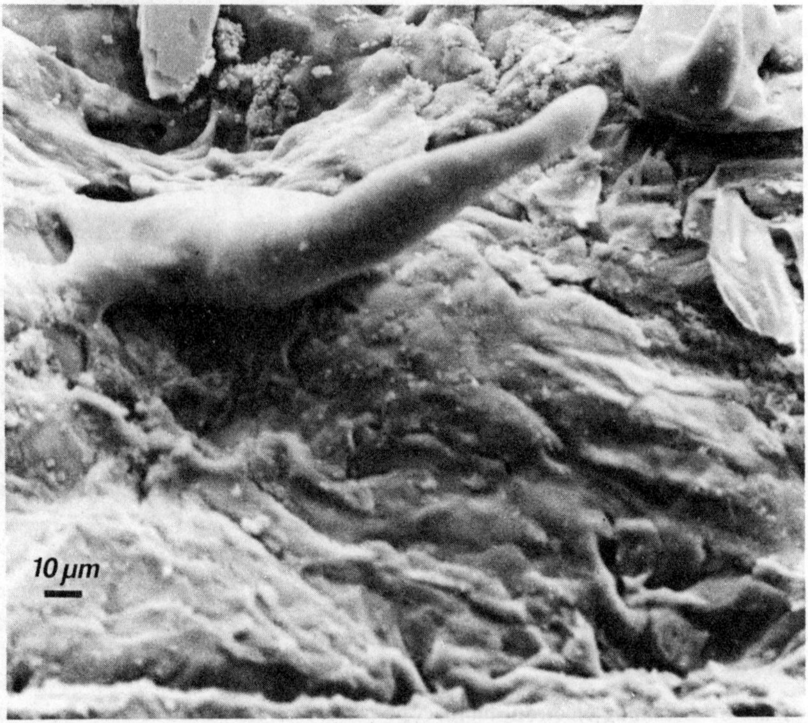

Plate 9 Scanning electron microscope picture of external surface of skin of *Rheobatrachus silus* showing a presumed sensory organ. (C. Miller)

to maintain a moist surface for gas exchange; and sometimes also in order to render the frog slippery if it is grabbed by an enemy.

B. *Granular Glands*—these secrete a white, creamy or even yellow fluid which contains toxic substances. These substances range from some which have an acrid smell or bitter taste to others that are extremely toxic and will even kill if taken into the mouth.

The skin of *Rheobatrachus* is particularly well endowed with glands (Plate 10). It is capable of producing such copious amounts of mucus that the frog can pop out of a naturalist's grip like a bar of wet soap. But the chemical nature of the granular secretions is not known as yet. At the time that the secretions of other Australian

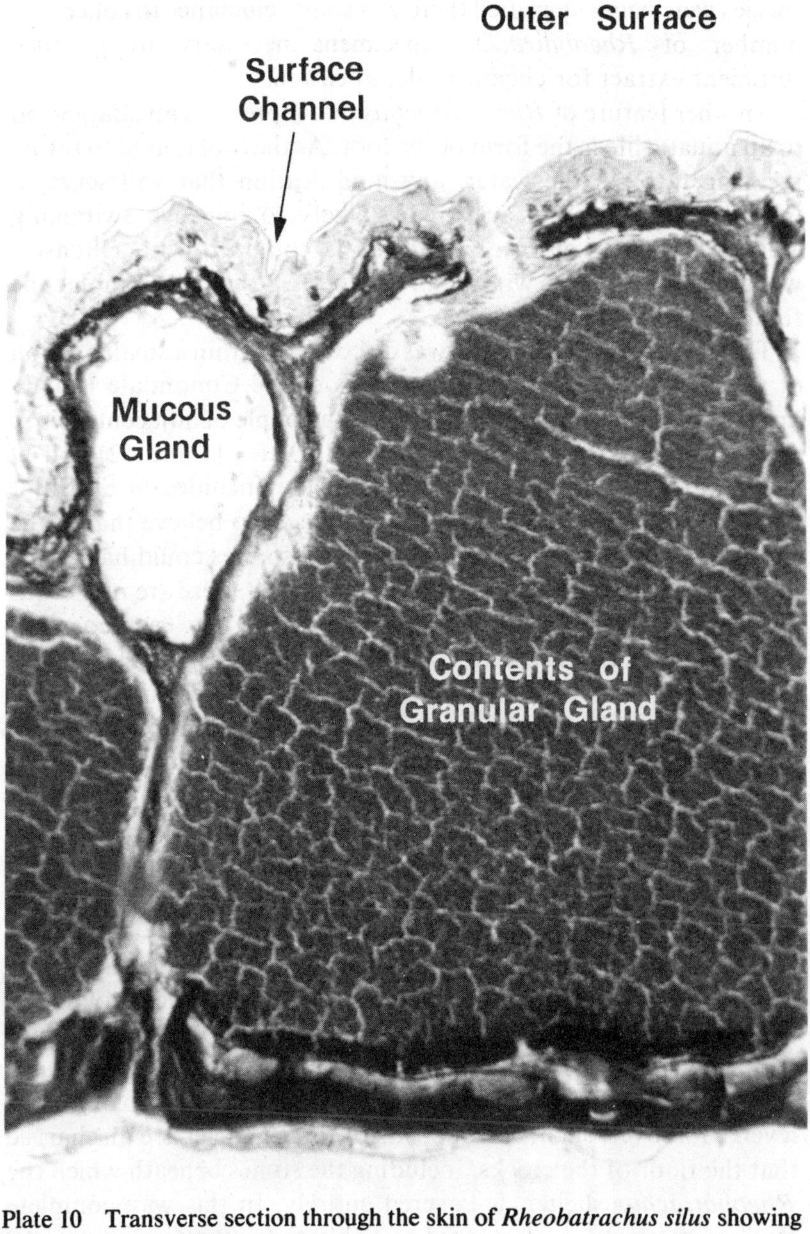

Plate 10 Transverse section through the skin of *Rheobatrachus silus* showing large glands. (C. Miller)

species were being identified there was some reluctance to collect the number of *Rheobatrachus* specimens necessary to produce sufficient extract for chemical identification.

Another feature of *Rheobatrachus* that represents an adaptation to an aquatic life is the form of the foot. As the foot is used to thrust the frog through the water, any modification that will serve to increase the foot's surface area is likely to improve swimming agility. The foot of *Rheobatrachus* is equipped with extensive webbing between the widely spread toes, so that it resembles the foot of a duck.

The Gastric Brooding Frog was discovered within a small portion of southeast Queensland in the creeks of the Conondale Ranges and of the Blackall Ranges, and also at a couple of adjacent sites in creeks draining these Ranges (Figure 2, Plates 11 and 12). All of these sites are within the Maroochy Shire that includes the Sunshine Coast towns and resorts. There is no reason to believe that at the time of the original discovery in 1973 the species could have been more widely distributed than it is today. In fact there are numerous populations of frogs of other species along the east coast of Australia that are restricted to very narrow zones. Some of these populations are so small that they are now vulnerable to extinction. For some species, the decline in population was probably due to huge climatic swings which decimated their numbers and destroyed the type of environment to which they are now restricted. European Man then took matters a step further by destroying the forests and by clearing and draining land for pastoral purposes. *Rheobatrachus* thus lives on an ecological tightrope and is now close to complete extinction.

It is certainly disturbing to find that the area in which *Rheobatrachus* was last seen is constantly being depleted of native hardwoods (Plate 13) by forestry contractors, with consequent damage to water quality in the creeks which were previously occupied by the frogs. This damage includes the alteration of the pH level. Moreover, such vast deposits of fine particles are discharged that the floor of the creeks, including the stones beneath which the *Rheobatrachus* shelter, is covered entirely. In this way complete sections of creek are destroyed as habitats for the frog.

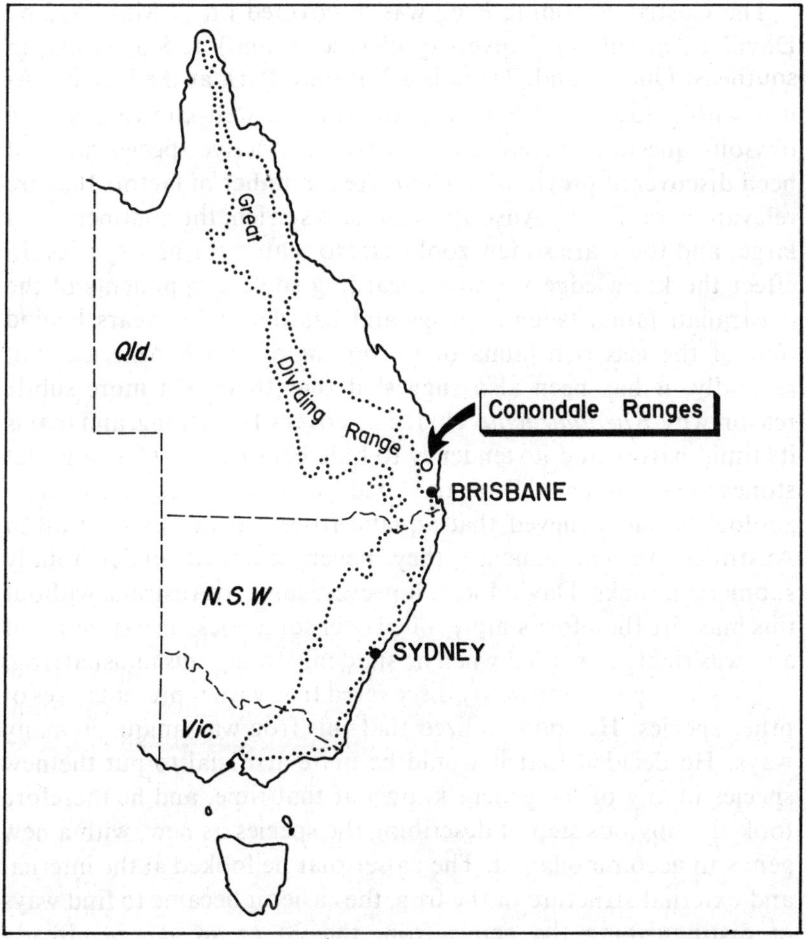

Figure 2 Location of the Connondale Ranges: the area to which *Rheobatrachus silus* is now confined.

But forestry is not the only cause of the silting of creeks. When the world price of gold rose substantially a few years ago, for instance, prospectors in Brisbane ran wild and panning for gold in the rich Conondales led to the damming of many sections of the creeks. These activities were sufficiently extensive to produce major deterioration in water quality by stirring up debris, silts and waste from the floor of pools.

The Gastric Brooding Frog was discovered on 17 May 1972 by David Liem (of the University of Queensland) at Kondalilla, in southeast Queensland. There is a National Park at the locality. As it is within 150 km of Brisbane, the site is a well-known one. The obvious question therefore is why this distinctive species had not been discovered previously. There are a number of factors that are relevant here. Firstly Australia's fauna is so rich, the continent is so large, and there are so few zoologists to search for new species. In effect the knowledge we have regarding some components of the Australian fauna (such as frogs and lizards) is 100 years behind that of the less rich fauna of Europe or of North America. But secondly, it has been also suggested that there is a more subtle reason why *Rheobatrachus* eluded discovery for so long, and that is its timid nature and its tendency to hide beneath boulders and flat stones in stream beds. Prior to David Liem's discovery, Australian zoologists had believed that aquatic frogs did not exist at all in Australia. In consequence they never searched under totally submerged rocks. David Liem, however, came to Australia without this bias. He therefore simply rolled over some rocks in a stream bed and was richly rewarded when he suddenly found this unusual frog.

Liem compared the newly discovered frog with representatives of other species. He soon realized that this frog was unique in many ways. He decided that it would be quite artificial to put the new species in any of the genera known at that time, and he therefore took the obvious step of describing the species as new, with a new genus to accommodate it. The closer that he looked at the internal and external structure of the frog, the easier it became to find ways of distinguishing the genus from the 20 or so genera already recognized in Australia. Liem thus named the new genus *Rheobatrachus* from the Latin words 'rheos' meaning stream, and 'batrachus' meaning frog. The species name *silus* literally means 'pugnosed' and it refers to the blunt snout.

The scientific paper which announced the discovery of this new frog was published in the *Memoirs of the Queensland Museum* issued on 30 June 1973. At that stage nothing was known of its life history. Liem wrote that 'egg masses and tadpoles are unknown'. There was no reason to suspect that the frog's development was in any way unusual. The excitement which was created by the discovery of *R. silus* was because of its retention of a number of anatomical features exhibited elsewhere in the world by species thought to be 'primitive'. It was thus inferred that *R. silus* retained some features characteristic of ancestral frogs. Hence the big question was whether it was a significant relic that had survived in Australia.

Less than five months after Liem's paper had been published, Chris Corben of Brisbane made the first observation which led to the discovery that the reproduction of *R. silus* was more bizarre than its appearance. On 4 November 1973 he had collected a large female frog and placed her in an aquarium where he could watch her behaviour. Nineteen days later he decided to transfer her to another aquarium. After rocks and other material in the tank had been removed the frog became agitated, swimming rapidly around and seeking a place in which she could hide. She then rose to the surface of the water, opened her mouth and vomited up six live tadpoles!

Such an extraordinary observation was hard to believe. (In fact, its acceptance by the scientific community at large probably took place only in 1981, when the first photographs of the young emerging through the frog's mouth were published.) There had been no tadpoles in the tank in which the adult frog had been housed. The tadpoles themselves were unusual in that they were unable to swim properly, and they did not survive.

The most likely explanation of Corben's observations was that *R. silus* had reproductive habits very similar to those of the *Rhinoderma darwini* of South America—namely that the adult was a male and that the tadpoles had been carried in the vocal sac beneath the throat. It so happened that I had made a special study of vocal sacs, including that of *Rhinoderma darwini.* So I was invited to join Corben and his colleague Glen Ingram in the study of *Rheobatrachus.*

The decision was taken to wait until the tadpoles had completed their development into young frogs, and then to preserve the adult with the babies still in the vocal sac. We reasoned, quite correctly, that only the presence of the young inside the body of the parent would convince anyone that this phenomenal biological event was not an elaborate hoax.

Observations on the adult frog were therefore increased. As the young grew, the frog became more bloated and its centre of gravity shifted. Gradually it lost the ability to hang horizontally in the water and instead it was suspended vertically. The movements of the developing young could be seen clearly as bulges vibrating upon the body wall.

Finally on 11 December (37 days after the capture of the adult frog) a baby frog was found swimming beside the parent in the aquarium. It was removed and two days later two more juveniles were found. Reluctantly the decision was taken to preserve the parent, but when it was grasped it rapidly vomited the remainder of the clutch of young.

The parent frog was preserved and posted to me in Adelaide so that I could examine the vocal sac. I prepared the dissection as carefully as a diamond cutter who was about to split a valuable stone, being extremely conscious of the unique nature of the specimen under my microscope.

I gently cut the skin covering the throat to reveal the muscles underneath, and was amazed to find that there was nothing special about them at all. I had anticipated that the muscles would be distended hugely in the manner of the *Rhinoderma* frogs. I looked inside the mouth and could not find any apertures to the vocal sac; and when I cut into the muscles I discovered that there was no vocal sac present. It did not make any sense at all, because males of almost all species of frogs have vocal sacs. And then the reason for the absence of a sac became obvious, when I looked into the body cavity. There I could clearly see the reproductive organs of a female.

Of even greater significance, however, was the huge size of the stomach. I realized that the only place in which the babies could have been brooded was inside the stomach. This was the first creature in the entire Animal Kingdom able to convert its stomach into a brooding chamber.

CHAPTER 4

Life in the Stomach

Ten years after the discovery of gastric brooding it is still not known whether it is the eggs or the young tadpoles that enter the mother's stomach, let alone how they find their way into it. But this void in our knowledge is not for the want of trying. Field studies carried out by Glen Ingram have failed to observe the crucial event. There occurred a similar lack of success with a captive colony which was maintained at the University of Adelaide (Plate 14). All that we know then is that the young reach the stomach unharmed.

Characteristically, almost all frogs capture food items with their tongue. They do not chew their food but swallow it whole. So the *R. silus* mother could presumably take the young into her mouth upon her tongue, but in *R. silus* the tongue is very poorly developed. Alternatively, the tadpoles may be swallowed after hatching. In the case of the *Rhinoderma darwini* of Chile the tadpoles swim into the open mouth of the parent and wriggle into the vocal sac through the apertures on the floor of the mouth. Similarly, in the case of the Australian marsupial frog *Assa darlingtoni* the tadpoles swim to the father and then push their way into his hip pockets. Hence if entry into the stomach of *R. silus* is an active process on the part of the tadpoles, the mother need only open her mouth. Like the adults of the two other species, she may take no other role in their entry into her body.

All that is known about the development of the tadpoles of *Rheobatrachus* and about their life in the mother's stomach results from two chance occurrences in which tadpoles have been born prematurely. The first occasion was the one described on page 29, when the captive mother disturbed by Chris Corben expelled six tadpoles. Then, in December 1978, a female which was distended

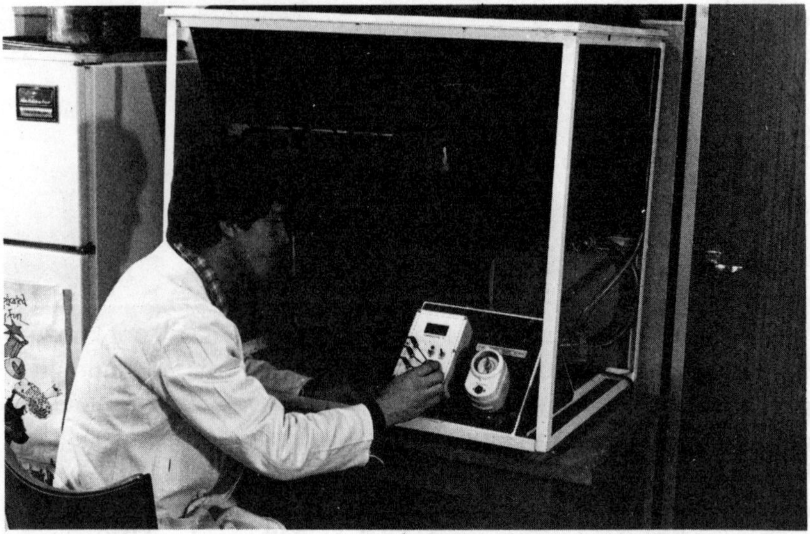

Plate 14 **Frog tank designed to house colony of *Rheobatrachus silus*. Chris Miller is operating a sensor that monitors temperatures at different sites in the tank at the back. The frogs are viewed through the portholes. (P. Kempster)**

with young was delayed in transit during her flight by air from Brisbane to Adelaide and, upon arrival, she vomited up 26 tadpoles. These tadpoles were maintained alive in the laboratory and they were eventually reared to young frogs. They provided a unique opportunity to observe developmental processes that would normally take place deep within the mother's stomach and hence that would be invisible to any observer.

An example of the earliest tadpole yet seen is shown in Plate 15. In its general form it consists of a large cream sphere with a small head, short tail and small developing limbs. In order to appreciate and assess its unique features we have to be aware of the progress of development in other species.

Although the development in any animal is a continuous process of change in structure and size, it is possible to divide the period of development into a series of distinct parts. In the case of a butterfly, for instance, the developmental span is a series of four readily recognized stages: egg, caterpillar (larva), chrysalis (pupa) and adult butterfly. In a sense, a frog's development can also be divided into

Above: Plate 1 A ground-dwelling toad, *Bufo marinus.* (B. Stankewytsch-Janusch)

Right: Plate 2 *Arenophyrne rotunda:* a head-first burrower found in coastal sandhills. (M. Davies)

Below: Plate 3 A burrowing water-holding frog *Cyclorana longpipes,* enclosed in its dry, transparent cocoon. On the front of the head the cocoon has lifted away from the underlying skin. (P. Kempster)

Above: Plate 4 A slender tree-frog, *Litoria olongburensis* (B. Stankewytsch-Janusch)

Right: Plate 7 Adult *Rheobatrachus silus*. (B. Stankewytsch-Janusch)

Below: Plate 11 One of the creeks of the Connondale Ranges

Left: Plate 12 Home for the Gastric Brooding Frog

Below: Plate 13 Rainforest logging

Bottom: Plate 15 Prematurely born tadpoles of *Rheobatrachus silus*. (P. Kempster)

Above: Plate 17 Oral birth. (D. Caville)

Right: Plate 18 Oral birth. (D. Caville)

Below: Plate 21 Advertisement for the Project Frog Appeal. (P. Kempster)

the stages of egg, tadpole (larva) and frog. But this broad classification is inadequate because the changes in development from an egg to a tadpole can be witnessed, unlike a butterfly larva emerging from an egg. Similarly, whereas the change of state from larva to butterfly is hidden from view inside the pupa wall, the tadpole's changes to convert it into a frog can be clearly seen.

Even if the structural changes in the development of a frog seem to be a continuum rather than a process punctuated by clear-cut and major alterations to the form of the individual, there remains a scheme for recognizing the attainment of particular steps in the developmental process. This scheme consists of noting the first appearance of particular features, or specified changes in proportions. The steps are termed stages and one of the most widely used staging tables is the one produced by K. L. Gosner in the USA in 1960 (Figure 3).

There are two major differences between what is known of the development of the *R. silus* tadpole and a tadpole that swims in water. The aquatic tadpole has a long, coiled intestine which appears black largely because of the food and silt packed inside it. In contrast, the tadpole of *R. silus* lives on its yolk and so lacks mouthparts and a coiled intestine. In consequence, its body retains the cream colour of the yolk. The second point of difference is that the tail of an aquatic tadpole is very well developed and under fine control to permit efficient movement in water, whereas the tail of *R. silus* is not so well developed.

There are many species of frogs throughout the world (but mainly in the tropics) that do not have aquatic tadpoles. Instead they equip their young with large yolk reserves, thus giving them a degree of independence. Some tadpoles are carried by their parents in specially developed skin pouches, e.g. the numerous marsupial frogs of South America. Quite commonly, the tadpoles that develop on land inside the egg membranes ('direct development') or in marsupial pouches are equipped with special respiratory organs. The marsupial frogs generally develop paired, bell-shaped gills (Figure 1c, page 19) for respiratory purposes. Moreover, the elaborate development of blood vessels in the tail of a New Guinea species which lays its eggs on land (Figure 1b, page 19) clearly indicates that

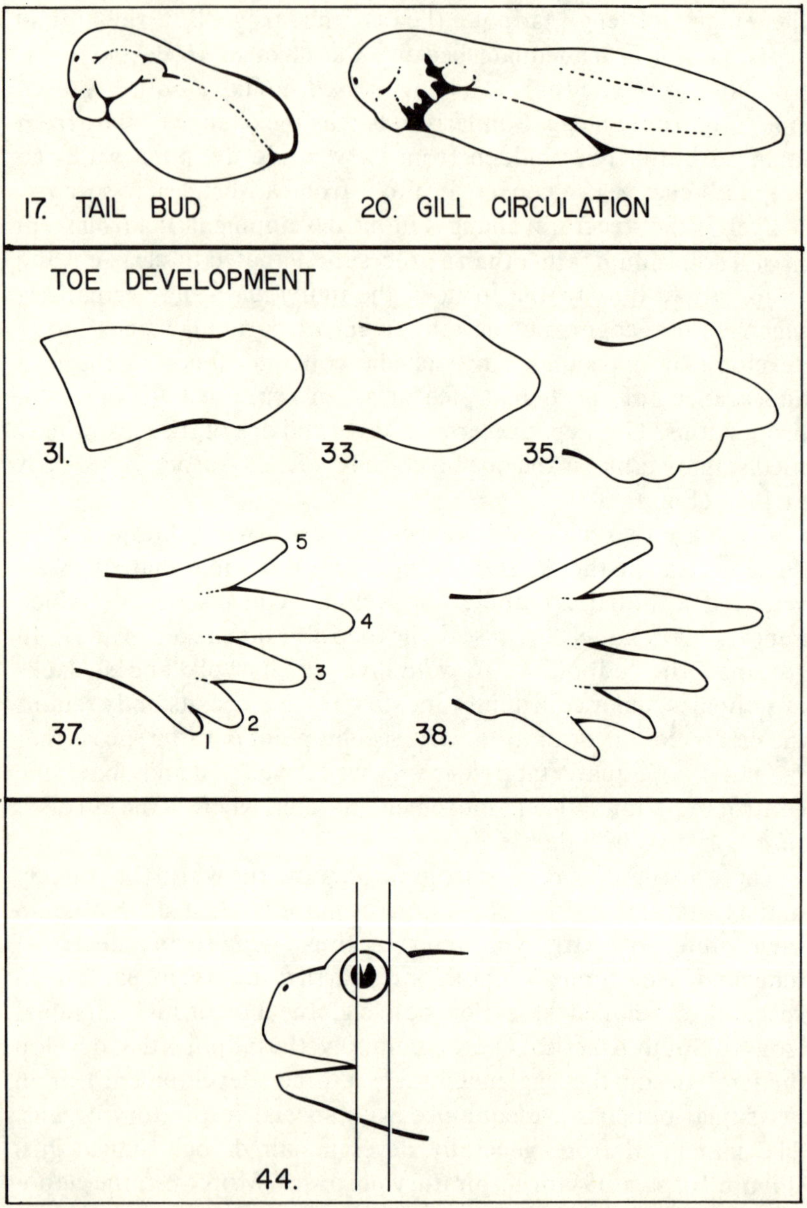

Figure 3 Selected stages from the tadpole staging tables developed by K. L. Gosner in 1960.

in that species at least the tail could serve as a major respiratory organ for gas exchange.

Consequently it is a source of surprise to discover that the tadpoles of *R. silus* in the mother's stomach do not possess any supplementary respiratory surface at all. No doubt they absorb oxygen and eliminate carbon dioxide at the skin surface in the manner of other tadpoles, but they evidently do so without the need for increased development of the blood vessels.

As the young increase in size in the mother's stomach, her stomach becomes more and more distended, squashing her other internal organs and eventually preventing her from inflating her lungs. The X-ray print shown in Plate 16 was taken approximately two weeks before the birth of the young, and even at that time the stomach can be seen to occupy most of the body cavity.

Plate 16 X-ray print of a *Rheobatrachus silus* mother carrying tadpoles in her stomach. (R. McDonald)

Despite the cramped conditions in the stomach the tadpoles can move a little. In fact movement can set off a chain reaction so that the whole distended skin covering the mother's stomach ripples with movement.

As the tadpoles develop functional arms and legs the mother becomes even larger, and the occasional piston-like movements of the tadpoles' knees and elbows upon her stomach wall can be observed quite readily. But if the mother is conscious of the movements she gives no sign of it!

It is not known just how long the young remain in the stomach. Tadpoles born prematurely at the University of Adelaide and reared successfully outside the mother's stomach took 42 days to complete their development from tadpoles to juvenile frogs. I estimate that the tadpoles were two to three weeks old when the premature birth occurred. Thus the tadpole's span in the stomach from the egg stage to the end of development is probably at least eight weeks.

CHAPTER 5

Oral Birth

The first observation in 1973 of baby frogs emerging through the mouth of the mother took the observers completely by surprise. It was all over in a couple of seconds. The mother simply opened her mouth wide, contracted her body muscles, and blew the babies out of her mouth like cannon balls. They literally flew through the air. It was not until 1979 that natural birth by an unrestrained mother was observed, and that photographs were obtained of babies emerging from the mouth of a mother held in my hand.

We do not know how the mother becomes aware that the babies are fully formed and therefore ready to be born. The ability of the babies to feed is probably the most important factor to be considered. This depends upon the completion of development of the gut so that it is an open tube able to digest food and to eliminate waste material in the form of faeces. Do the babies increase their movements in the stomach, or is there some other signal to the mother to initiate the special behaviour which is associated with the birth of her young? This is just one of many intriguing questions that remain to be answered.

From the few observations that have been made, it seems that the births of babies are spaced out over several days. For example, in February 1979 one frog gave birth to 25 babies over a period of six days, and most of them were born at night.

The birth procedure is fascinating. Normally the mother slowly rises to the surface of the water, opens her mouth wide, and dilates the oesophagus. Because the stomach is under great tension this dilation results in one or two babies popping up into the mouth, where they sit upon the tongue (Plate 17). The mother keeps her jaws wide apart, waiting for the babies to step or hop out (Plate 18).

But if a baby is reluctant to leave, the mother closes her jaws and with great effort swallows to push it back into the stomach. The mother then sinks to the bottom of the water and remains inactive until she wishes to release more babies, when she once more rises to the surface and repeats the procedure.

CHAPTER 6

Changing a stomach to a uterus

The frog stomach conforms to the generalized pattern of structure of other vertebrate animals. Thus, it lies principally on the left side of the body and tends to be convex on the left side and concave on the right side. The stomach is connected to the mouth cavity by a very short oesophagus. It ends at a constricted area, termed the pylorus, where there is a region of change from stomach tissue to the duodenum, which leads in turn to the small intestine (Figure 4).

When the stomach is empty the inner surface bears several large ridges, running along its entire length and separated by grooves. When distended with food the expansion of the stomach seems to be uniform over the entire organ, unless the objects that have been swallowed are particularly large.

Frogs tend to eat anything that moves and which is small enough to pass between their jaws. Hence large frogs will eat mice and even small birds if they get the chance. The critical factor is where they live and the nature of the potential prey that occur in that region. As frogs do not chew their food but swallow items whole, gross distension of the stomach can occur quite frequently.

The glands that discharge into the stomach differ in type along its length. At the point at which the oesophagus merges into the stomach is a narrow zone just 1–2 mm wide where cells secreting pepsinogen are to be found. Throughout the main body or fundus of the stomach are glands containing oxyntic cells (sometimes termed parietal cells) which secrete hydrochloric acid. In contrast the pyloric region contains cells that secrete mucus.

In a transverse section through the wall of the fundic region of the stomach of a normal *Rheobatrachus* (Plate 19), the various tissues appear to be comparable to those found in other species of frogs.

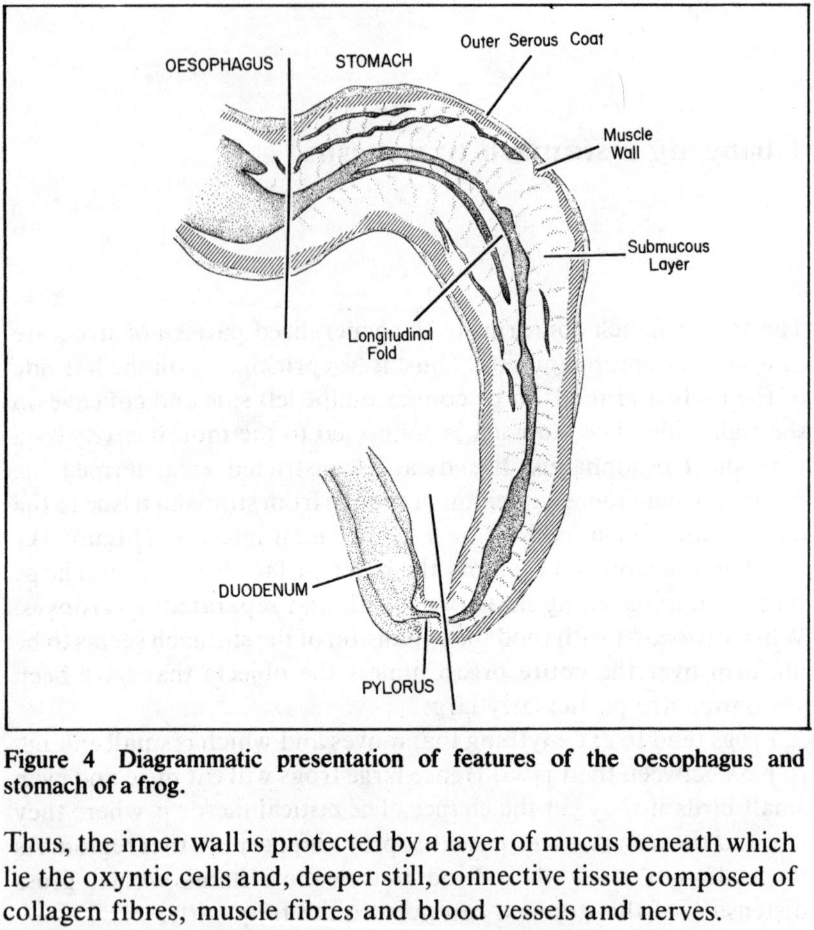

Figure 4 Diagrammatic presentation of features of the oesophagus and stomach of a frog.

Thus, the inner wall is protected by a layer of mucus beneath which lie the oxyntic cells and, deeper still, connective tissue composed of collagen fibres, muscle fibres and blood vessels and nerves.

The process of breakdown of food is a finely controlled chemical and physical process. The hormones gastrin and histamine stimulate the release of hydrochloric acid by the oxyntic cells to convert pepsinogen into a corrosive substance termed pepsin which erodes away at the food material, whilst the stomach contents are moved and churned up by strong waves of muscular contraction moving in any direction across the stomach wall, constantly pushing the contents from one place to another.

The stomach of *Rheobatrachus* is therefore no more suitable for use as a uterus than the stomach of any other frog, or in fact of any

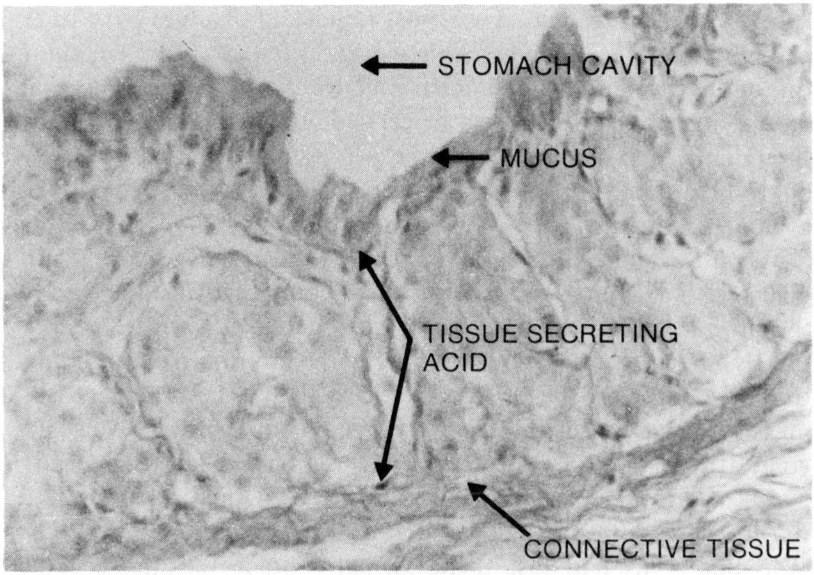

Plate 19 Low power section through the wall of the stomach of a normal (non-brooding) *Rheobatrachus silus*. (D. Caville)

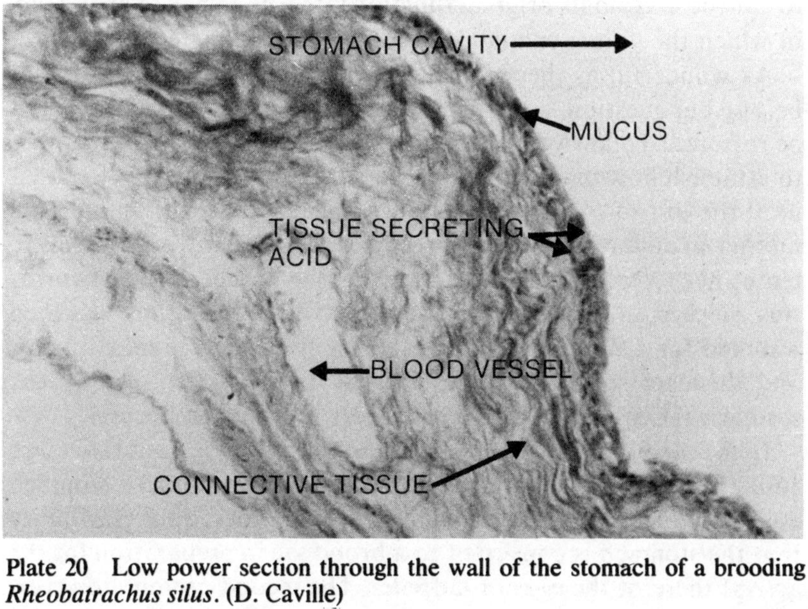

Plate 20 Low power section through the wall of the stomach of a brooding *Rheobatrachus silus*. (D. Caville)

other vertebrate animal. Two most important changes have to be brought about for the conversion to occur. Firstly, a rapid switching off of the production and release of the hydrochloric acid that would digest the babies must be carried out. Secondly, an equally rapid halt must bring to close any muscular activity that, if it continued after the babies had been swallowed, would bruise or even crush them.

When the wall of the stomach of a *Rheobatrachus* that has just given birth to young was sectioned and compared with the wall of the normal structure, many differences could be seen (Plate 20). Firstly, there is the obvious thinning of the total wall, reduced now to a small fraction of its former size. This had been achieved by massive reduction of the layer containing the secretory cells (the connective tissue zone of collagen fibres had in fact thickened). Muscle fibres were hard to locate, and electron microscopy showed that the muscle layer had been stretched to such an extent that the individual cells had lost their normal contact and had become instead separated from one another.

The net result of all of these structural changes to the stomach is to convert it from its original function into a plain bag or brood sac, in which the young can complete their development in safety.

As wonderful as these structural and functional changes might be, the big question lay in whether normal stomach function could be restored. To answer this matter, X-rays were taken of a mother to establish how many young remained in her stomach. We waited until the last of the babies had been born, and then we placed the mother in an aquarium containing a pot of 10 tasty mealworms to tempt her to feed. At regular intervals the number of mealworms was checked. After four days, it began to fall. The mother was then watched for a further three days whilst she ate more mealworms, and then her stomach was examined. To our great surprise the stomach tissues had almost completely returned to normal.

In the early days of our investigation we had recognized that there could be two ways in which such changes in the mother's stomach could be brought about. Firstly, we had considered the possibility that the stomach is converted to a brood sac in preparation for the arrival there of the eggs or tadpoles. The second option, however, was that the stomach was normal at the time that the young were swallowed, and that the eggs, tadpoles and young frgos secreted a substance that switched off the production of hydrochloric acid to bring about the other changes.

Of the two options, the first was the most appealing, if only because we all judge parental behaviour in terms of the ultimate reactions which are manifested by responsible and caring human beings. However, this first hypothesis (a pre-prepared stomach) was also the more complex.

This is because the range of dates on which births had been observed in the laboratory suggested a breeding season of at least two months' duration. The females thus cannot determine in advance when climatic and other factors will affect the males sufficiently for them to call and so become involved in the mating procedure. As a result it was just not possible to envisage that the female could be active for a long period with a non-functional stomach before the swallowing of the young. The more likely hypothesis, therefore, was that the young themselves brought about the structural changes by secreting a protective substance against gastric secretion.

CHAPTER 7

Project Frog

A considerable amount of information on *Rheobatrachus* has been obtained as the result of a research program based in Adelaide, South Australia. This program brought together local scientists from a variety of fields. It is an excellent example of what is termed multi-disciplinary research, in which investigators with different spheres of interest pool their ideas and resources to solve complex problems. There is something really exciting about being involved in such a program because each of the contributors looks at the overall problem in a different way. Also, results obtained from one area can show that it would be profitable to change the whole direction of research altogether, and employ totally different techniques.

The research group was formed for a specific reason. The ability to halt for a period the production of hydrochloric acid in the stomach, and later to return the stomach's functions to normal, is an attribute that would be greatly beneficial in human sufferers of gastric ulcers. We therefore wished to discover the identity of the inhibitor of acid secretion.

Obviously, determining such things as how the mother frog fails to digest her young when they enter her stomach requires all sorts of expertise. We can use zoology for basic studies on the animal and to work out how the habit of gastric brooding could have evolved. Gastroenterology enables us to anticipate the changes that are needed in the function of the stomach. Pharmacology is needed in order to devise tests that can detect the presence of an inhibitor of gastric acid production in the stomach, and eventually in order to identify that substance. And biochemistry permits us to carry out chemical tests to isolate the substance, and to confirm its physical structure. Then there is also a need for information on just how the cells of the tissue of the stomach wall are affected—and this calls for the collaboration of an expert in electron microscopy.

No-one could have sat down at the beginning of the research on *Rheobatrachus* and anticipated the various research needs in much detail. The program grew in fits and starts as new facts emerged and future needs became clear.

The first part of the research involved trying to find the substance which, when secreted by the eggs and tadpoles, had the ability to switch off the production of hydrochloric acid in the cells of the stomach wall. The Utah Foundation generously donated $21,000 for the work. This project required an apparatus termed a Ussing Chamber, which consists of two transparent and excavated cylinders of a material called Lucite. A sheet of stomach is held tightly between the two cylinders, thus creating a complete barrier between them. The stomach is kept alive by being immersed in an oxygenated fluid which supplies its mineral, salt and energy needs.

We used stomachs of a pest species: the cane toad *Bufo marinus* which was introduced into Australia in 1935 and is now extremely abundant. Because *Bufo marinus* is considered by many people to be a pest, it seems somehow fitting that it should play a valuable role in scientific research.

The Ussing Chamber is constructed in such a way that the amount of hydrochloric acid secreted by the living stomach inside it can be detected and measured, by means of an automatic titrator and a pH meter. In addition, it is possible to add drugs and extracts into the apparatus, and to determine whether they have any effect upon the normal rate of acid production.

We first attempted to demonstrate that when inside the Ussing Chamber the prepared stomach would respond to substances known to affect the rate of gastric secretion in other animals. For example, histamine is a drug which stimulates acid production in animals, while the drug Cimetadine decreases it. In early experiments the isolated *Bufo marinus* stomach responded perfectly, enabling us therefore to test for the presence of an inhibitor in the secretions produced by the young *Rheobatrachus*. At that time, we did not have any tadpoles to test. But we did have several litres of aquarium water in which a prematurely born clutch (mentioned on page 32) had been reared two years previously, as the water had been stored deep-frozen.

It certainly seems an odd idea to store used aquarium water rather than to pour it down the sink. The reason for keeping it was based on nothing more than a hunch. Whilst watching the prematurely born tadpoles we noticed that they released from their mouths tiny, transparent, hair-like strands of mucus. These strands accumulated in the water to such an extent that we had first thought that the water was being contaminated with particles of fluff carried in the air. We soon realized there had to be some purpose behind the release of so much mucus, and one possibility was that it contained the substance that inhibited gastric secretion. Deep-freezing was therefore intended to prevent any inhibitor present from decomposing.

When we wanted to test the frozen aquarium water upon a stomach in the Ussing Chamber we firstly concentrated the water by freeze-drying. This is a process that extracts the water and leaves behind other matter that is dissolved in it. It thus involves removing the water whilst maintaining a low temperature, so as to prevent the breakdown that would occur if it was allowed to warm up.

From the powder which was obtained, a solution was prepared that was much more concentrated than the original one. When a little of this concentrated aquarium water was added to the Ussing Chamber, the rate of hydrochloric acid production fell dramatically, thus confirming that the tadpole could indeed be responsible for switching off the gastric secretions of the mother.

Research on *Rheobatrachus silus* has always attracted considerable attention from all sections of the media. In particular, questions have centred upon whether knowledge of how the mother frog switches off gastric secretion can be applied to a cure for human sufferers of gastric ulcers. If the mother's stomach can be given a rest from acid production, will not a similar rest enable a gastric ulcer to heal? Publicity about this particular aspect has led to what is now termed 'Project Frog'.

'Project Frog' was launched in 1982 by a committee involved in promoting awareness and pride of their home state amongst the residents of South Australia. This committee decided to publicize activities that were uniquely South Australian, and one of the scientific topics selected for promotion was the research on *Rheobatrachus silus*. In consequence, as our need for funds to support our research began to grow, the Savings Bank of South Australia came to our aid with a proposal to raise money on our behalf. The name 'Project F.R.O.G.' (Funds for Research Of Gastric-acids) was coined for the venture (Plate 21). The appeal was launched on 25 August 1982 by the then Premier of South Australia, the Honourable David Tonkin, and the Savings Bank of South Australia opened the fund with a donation.

The laboratory investigation continued and focused upon identifying the inhibitor of gastric secretion in the aquarium water. Various analytical techniques demonstrated beyond any reasonable doubt that the inhibitor is a member of a group of substances known as prostaglandins. Prostaglandins are found in most of the different kinds of cells present in the body. They are known to have a wide range of effects upon processes within cells. Thus in a review in the *New Scientist* (October 1982) Omar Sattaur wrote that 'no one gets tired of studying prostaglandins, and excitement about research on them seldom wanes. The more work that is carried out in the area, the more diverse and crucial their functions appear to be.'

Prostaglandins are notoriously unstable substances. Therefore, if they are to keep the stomach in a non-secreting state, either a continuous supply has to be produced, or else prostaglandins in the stomach are somehow stabilized. The matter is only just being investigated, and whatever the answer proves to be, the fact remains that the frog exhibits complete control of hydrochloric acid production without any known ill effects. Normal functions are restored within a few days of the departure of the last baby.

Many aspects of the changes occurring inside the mother, and of the way in which the babies obtain oxygen and excrete waste and so on, remain entirely unknown. The normal difficulty of carrying out such research is now compounded by a recent disastrous drought which almost totally destroyed the frogs. The creeks and pools have dried up! Up until the time of writing (August 1983), no *Rheobatrachus* has been seen in the field for over two years, and the species is now recognized to be on the brink of extinction. Hopefully, in a remote creek there does remain a few individuals; and hopefully the species may survive and one day flourish once more. But if it fails to survive, then we will never properly understand the secrets of the Gastric Brooding Frog.

FURTHER READING

A. *Specific information on Rheobatrachus*

There is a technical book summarizing all that was then known about this frog:

Tyler, M. J. (1983) (Ed.) *The Gastric Brooding Frog* (Croom Helm, London and Canberra).

Since the completion of that manuscript two other papers have been published. The first is on changes to muscle cells in the stomach wall, and the second on the discovery that a prostaglandin is the inhibitor of gastric secretion:

Gibbins, I. F. and Tyler, M. J. (1983). 'Changes in the organisation of smooth muscle cells in the stomach of the gastric brooding frog, *Rheobatrachus silus*, during brooding.' *Cell and Tissue Research,* Vol. 231, pp. 451–6.

Tyler, M. J., Shearman, D. J. C., Franco, R., O'Brien, P., Seamark, R. F. and Kelly, R. (1983). 'Inhibition of gastric acid secretion in the gastric brooding frog, *Rheobatrachus silus*.' *Science*, Vol. 220, pp. 609–10.

B. *General references on frogs*

There are two books that provide guides to assist the identification of Australian frogs:

Barker, J. and Grigg, G. (1977). *A field guide to Australian Frogs* (Rigby, Adelaide).

Cogger, H. G. (1983). *Reptiles and Amphibians of Australia* (Revised Edition) (Reed, Sydney).

The first of these books is out of print but copies are obtainable in many libraries.

For general biological information about frogs see:

Tyler, M. J. (1982). *Frogs* (Amended Edition) (Collins, Sydney).

Two other books provide a broad coverage of the world's frog fauna:

Goin, C. J., Goin, O. B. and Zug, C. R. (1978). *Introduction to Herpetology* (3rd Edition) (W. H. Freeman, San Francisco).

Webb, J. E., Wallwork, J. A. and Elgood, J. H. (1981). *Guide to living amphibians* (Macmillan, London).

INDEX